FESTIVAL FU
for the Early Ye

HARVEST

- Fun activity ideas -
- Photocopiable resources -
- Information on customs and beliefs -

SCHOLASTIC **Jenni Tavener**

CREDITS

Author
Jenni Tavener

Editor
Susan Elliot

Assistant Editor
Victoria Lee

Series Designer
Catherine Mason

Designer
Erik Ivens

Cover Illustration
Catherine Mason

Illustrations
Jenny Tulip

Text © Jenni Tavener 2005
© 2005 Scholastic Ltd

Published by Scholastic Ltd
Villiers House
Clarendon Avenue
Leamington Spa
Warwickshire
CV32 5PR

www.scholastic.co.uk

Printed by Bell & Bain

2 3 4 5 6 7 8 9   6 7 8 9 0 1 2 3 4

British Library Cataloguing-in-Publication Data
A catalogue record for this book is available from the British Library.

ISBN 0-439-96490-3
ISBN 9780439964906

Acknowledgement
Qualifications and Curriculum Authority for the use of extracts from the QCA/DfEE document *Curriculum Guidance for the Foundation Stage* © 2000 Qualifications and Curriculum Authority.

CONTENTS

HARVEST

INTRODUCTION

Celebrating festivals with young children

Festivals and celebrations are an exciting theme to explore with young children. They offer scope for children to gain an awareness of a range of cultures and traditions, and experience a wide variety range of activities. Many festivals are associated with a particular season, and this provides opportunities for cross-curricular learning across many different themes. It is important that children understand and feel involved in the preparations and celebrations for any festival and the activities in this book provide opportunities for every member of your setting to join in and make a valued contribution.

Multicultural awareness

The celebrations associated with Harvest provide a good insight into beliefs that span many cultures and religions. For example, caring for others less fortunate than us, sharing what we have and thanking God for His gifts. Different religions may celebrate in different styles and they may tell different stories or recall different historical events. However, there are obvious universal elements, such as decorating places of worship, sharing gifts, getting together with family and friends and sharing special meals.

Involving parents and the community

It is important to involve parents and carers as much as possible with the themes, activities, celebrations and special events organised for the children in your setting. A Harvest festival is an ideal starting point as the traditions associated with this celebration lend themselves to community involvement. You can involve parents, carers, grandparents and relatives in helping their children to gain an awareness of giving and sharing in many different ways. For example, invite parents into your setting in spring or summer to help the children plant flowers or vegetables specifically for the Harvest festival. Encourage families to assist with the preparations for a Harvest festival service by helping their children decorate a box or basket to fill with fresh fruit and vegetables for a display. Invite relatives into your setting to make bread with the children to take to the festival. Suggest that they help their children sort out some tinned or packet food from cupboards at home to add to the harvest display.

How to use this book

The book begins with background information about the Harvest festival, with details such as dates, religious beliefs, customs and traditions. This is followed by a set of poster notes, offering ideas on how to use the posters with young children, including points to talk about, things to observe, and questions to ask. The planning page shows a topic web that explains how the main activities link up with the six Areas of Learning. The photocopiable pages include two stories suitable for reading aloud to the children and a collection of new action rhymes and songs all related to the theme of Harvest.

HARVEST
BACKGROUND INFORMATION AND PLANNING

Dates
- Late summer and early autumn is Harvest time.
- Lugnasad was a Celtic festival of 'Fruitfulness'. It was celebrated on 1 August. During this festival, people offered food to the Gods and celebrated with festivals and fairs. The festival of Lugnasad was later adapted by the Christian church and called 'Lammas'.
- Lammas Day was celebrated when the first wheat had been cut at the beginning of Harvest. The word 'Lammas' comes from an old English word, 'loaf-mass'. It was used to describe small loaves that were baked from the first wheat gathered in the local fields. These loaves were shared during the Communion service in church on 1 August.
- Michaelmas was a time for feasting and was celebrated on 29 September. It was when farmers were paid for their crops, and hired harvest labourers were no longer required because their work in the fields was complete.
- In the mid 1800s, people began to hold Harvest festivals at the end of the harvest, and this tradition still continues today.

Religious beliefs
- Harvest festival is a time when people thank God for the food that has been grown during the summer, and which will keep everyone fed during winter.
- People attend special Harvest services at local churches, taking gifts of food and flowers. Churches are decorated with specially-made Harvest loaves, baskets of fruit and vegetables, and sheaves of wheat.
- Harvest festivals are also held in schools, and children bring in gifts of flowers, fruit, vegetables and tinned goods. One of the most important parts of the Harvest festival service is the sharing and giving. After the church or school service, the gifts of food and flowers are given to local people in need.
- People of many religions across the world pray and give thanks for Harvest.

Customs and traditions
- The corn dolly is associated with the Harvest festival and, long ago, it was the custom for each farming community to make its own corn-dolly shape. Some people thought that a spirit lived hid in the last few sheaves of corn to be cut. They believed that if they made a corn dolly using these last bundles of corn, then they would keep the spirit alive, and the corn dolly would hold the spirit from one harvest to the next. At the end of winter, the corn dolly was often put in the soil with the new corn seeds in the hope of a good harvest the following year.
- The Harvest loaf is a traditional type of bread made in the shape of a sheaf of corn, and traditionally represents all the food that we eat. Often, a little mouse shape is added to the loaf before it is baked. This helps us to remember that it is not just humans that rely on a good harvest, but animals too.

BACKGROUND INFORMATION AND PLANNING

● Pearly kings and queens are associated with Harvest time and date back to the Victorian era. Originally, they sold fruit and vegetables from barrows in the streets of London. To brighten up their clothing, they sewed on pearl buttons, creating elaborate patterns such as flowers, fruit, stars, moons, diamonds, bells and place names. Harvest was a special time of year for these traders so, every year, Pearly princesses took bouquets of vegetables as 'thank you' offerings to the Harvest festival church service in St Martin-in-the-Fields in London. This tradition still exists today.

● American families celebrate the first good harvest of the Pilgrim Fathers with a special celebration called Thanksgiving. The Pilgrim Fathers were European people who sailed to North America on a ship called the Mayflower. They tried to make America their home, but this was difficult because they did not have enough food to eat. Local Native Americans helped the pilgrims achieve their first good harvest and the pilgrims held a great feast with the Native Americans to celebrate.

Celebrations

● 'Harvest-home' was an important part of the Harvest celebrations. Once the last field had been harvested, the farmers and hired labourers enjoyed a great feast or Harvest supper. In the times before farm machines such as combine harvesters, the workers had to do everything by hand. At the end of the harvest, the farmers and labourers could relax and enjoy the fruits of their labours. For many of the workers, the 'Harvest-home' was one of the best meals they had until Christmas.

Things to remember

● Before any Harvest activity that includes food or drink, check with families or carers for any allergies or dietary requirements.

● Remember to be sensitive to individual family circumstances.

Using the posters

● The first poster shows a colourful selection of Harvest produce Encourage the children's observation skills by asking questions such as, 'Can you see a sheaf of corn?'; 'What colour are the different cheeses?'; 'How many different-shaped loaves of bread can you find?'. Help the children to name and identify some of the familiar fruits and vegetables in the poster. Use information books and other reference sources to find out about less familiar items such as the traditional milk churn and the corn-dolly mobile.

● The second poster shows a farming scene at Harvest time. The land is green and lush and the farming equipment is modern. Encourage the children to describe the scene and to think about what the farmer might be harvesting. Discuss past and present farming methods, such as the changing role of horses and the introduction of machines. Talk about the weather conditions needed to create a thriving crop, then encourage the children to consider what might happen if the weather was not very good.

HARVEST
FESTIVAL PLANNER

CROSS-CURRICULAR IDEAS

Personal, social and emotional development

Be confident to try new activities, initiate ideas and speak in a familiar group.

Talk About
Begin the activity by talking about scarecrows and why farmers use them.

SCARECROW DRESSING

What you need
Three old hats, each with a sticky label attached showing a picture of one, two or three crows; three old jackets and three old pairs of trousers (labelled in the same way); three card discs showing one, two or three crows; a bag.

What to do
● Ask three children to sit together on the floor next to the pile of labelled jackets and trousers.
● The players should take turns to pick a disc from the bag. If, for example, they pick a card showing one crow, then they must collect and put on an item of clothing labelled with one crow. If there are no items labelled with one crow left, that player misses a go.
● Repeat until each player is dressed up as a scarecrow in one hat, jacket and pair of trousers.
● Give the children a copy each of 'The friendly scarecrow' photocopiable sheet on page 38 and encourage them to arrange the pictures in the correct order.

LOOK IN THE BARN

What you need
Two toy haystacks (or two blocks of yellow Lego); three large cardboard boxes; the song 'Round and round the hay barn' on page 35.

Preparation
Encourage the children to decorate the boxes to look like barns.

What to do
● Organise the children into two or more groups, each with three players.
● Ask the children to look away or shut their eyes as you hide the pretend haystacks under one of the barns.
● Encourage the first group of children to march around all three barns singing the rhyme 'Round and round the hay barn'.
● When the song is finished, invite each child to choose one barn to peep under.
● The child who finds the two haystacks is the winner. Encourage the winner to be sensitive to the feelings of the other two players by offering them one haystack each to hide underneath one of the barns for the next group to find.

Early Learning Goal
Have a developing awareness of their own needs, views and feelings and be sensitive to the needs, views and feelings of others.

Talk About
Discuss why it is important to play games fairly and to take turns.

CROSS-CURRICULAR IDEAS

Personal, social and emotional development

Early Learning Goal
Select and use activities and resources independently.

Talk About
Talk about traditional corn-dolly shapes, such as horseshoes, moons, crescents and ladies.

CORN DOLLY

What you need
White paper straws; stapler (adult use); colourful wide and narrow ribbon; pictures or samples of traditional corn dollies.

What to do
● Explain that people used to believe that making a corn dolly would help to bring a good harvest the following year.
● Help the children to twist or plait three paper straws together. An adult should secure each end of the twist or plait with a stapler.
● Repeat the process to make another plait, then help the children to join both twists or plaits together using wide colourful ribbon. Knot the ribbon to form a loop for hanging.
● Invite the children to decorate the other two 'free' ends with a small bow using narrow ribbon.
● Display the children's 'corn' dollies with books and pictures about the tradition.

LITTLE RED HEN

What you need
A copy of the story book *The Little Red Hen* (*Favourite Tales* series, Ladybird Books); role-play area.

What to do
● Read or tell the children the story of *The Little Red Hen*.
● Encourage the children to re-enact scenes from the story. For example: the Little Red Hen planting the grain while the other animals watch; reaping, threshing and milling the wheat while the other animal's sleep; kneading the dough and baking the bread while the other animals play; all of the animals wanting to eat the bread made by Little Red Hen!
● Let different children take turns to be the Little Red Hen. After a short while, sit down together and talk about the role-play. Discuss how the Little Red Hen felt, doing all of the hard work herself, and talk about ways in which the other animals should have helped. The children may be able to provide examples of how they can help others.

Early Learning Goal
Continue to be interested, excited and motivated to learn.

Talk About
Talk to the children about the difference between working hard and being lazy.

Further Ideas
● Extend the 'Scarecrow dressing' game on page 8 by using a 1 to 6 dice instead of discs and by labelling the clothes with pictures of two, four or six crows.
● Invite pairs of children to work together to play the 'Mr Scarecrow' game on page 39.
● Invite younger siblings into your setting to join in the 'Look in the barn' game on page 8. Ask the older children to help teach the rhyme and game to younger visitors.
● Reflect on the story of 'The Little Red Hen'. Invite the children to write a 'thank you' card to someone who they think works very hard at home.

Communication, language and literacy

Early Learning Goal Speak clearly and audibly with confidence and control and show awareness of the listener, for example by their use of conventions such as greetings, 'please' and 'thank you'.

Talk About Talk about the different people that we say 'thank you' to for our food. Explain that the rhyme could also be used as a prayer to thank God for the food that is gathered at Harvest time.

Early Learning Goal Know that print carries meaning and, in English, is read from left to right and top to bottom.

Talk About Talk about the gifts that people bring to a Harvest festival and the people that they are donated to.

'THANK YOU' PRAYER

What you need

A copy of the 'Harvest poem' photocopiable sheet on page 40 for each child; coloured pens and pencils; scissors; A4 mounting card; glue.

What to do

● Invite the children to join in with the rhyme entitled 'Thank you' on the photocopiable sheet.

● When you have read it through together a few times, encourage the children to discuss the rhyme. Ask questions, for example: 'Why are we thankful for sun and rain?'; 'Who do we need to thank for growing and gathering crops?'; 'Who should we thank for our food?'.

● If necessary, prompt with ideas such as farm workers, bakers and parents. Provide each child with a copy of the rhyme. Encourage them to decorate it using their own choice of colours, then cut out and mount the finished rhymes to display on the wall.

COLOURFUL GIFTS

What you need

For each child, a long strip of paper folded twice to make a zigzag booklet; scissors; coloured pens and pencils; real examples or pictures of traditional Harvest foods.

What to do

● Help the children to trim the edges of their zigzag booklet to create the shape of an old church roof.

● Encourage them to decorate the cover of their booklet to represent a church entrance.

● Using the pictures and objects for inspiration, invite the children to think of different-coloured Harvest gifts, such as 'Red apples', 'Orange flowers', 'Brown bread'. Encourage them to decorate each page of their zigzag booklet with a different-coloured picture. Help them to write the words in pencil underneath.

Red apples   Brown bread   Orange flowers

HARVEST
CROSS-CURRICULAR IDEAS

HARVEST RECIPES

What you need
Oatcake ingredients: 200g rolled oats, 75g butter, 75g golden syrup, 75g soft brown sugar; equipment: cooker (adult use), saucepan, plastic bowl, wooden spoon, baking tin; a copy of the 'Harvest recipe' photocopiable sheet on page 41 for each child; colouring materials.

Preparation
Check for food allergies and dietary requirements. Ask the children to wash their hands and put on aprons.

What to do
● An adult should melt the butter, syrup and sugar over a low heat. When cool, pour the mixture into a plastic bowl.
● Invite the children to stir the oats into the mixture. Spread the mixture into the base of a buttered tin, pressing down with the wooden spoon.
● Bake for 30 minutes at 180°C, 350°F or gas mark 4.
● Remove the oatcake from the oven and score it while it is still warm. Wait until it is cool to remove it from the tin.
● Give each child a copy of the 'Harvest recipe' photocopiable sheet. Encourage them to identify and colour in the ingredients and to write a simple version of the recipe on the lines.
● Secure the sheets together to create a booklet.

Early Learning Goal
Use their phonic knowledge to write simple regular words and make phonetically plausible attempts at more complex words.

Talk About
Discuss the ingredients in the Harvest recipe. Which ones do we associate with Harvest time?

IT'S HARVEST TIME TODAY!

What you need
A copy of the rhyme 'It's Harvest time today!' on page 35; paper; coloured pencils.

What to do
● Encourage the children to join in with the rhyme, to the well-known tune 'Sing a Song of Sixpence', counting down from five bales to one bale.
● Distribute the paper and coloured pencils and invite the children to illustrate scenes from the rhyme such as the corn growing, the bales of hay and the hay flying away.
● When they have finished their pictures help each child to write a simple label, caption or sentence to describe the pictures.
● Display the words and pictures on the wall with a copy of the rhyme.

Early Learning Goal
Write their own names, and other things such as labels and captions and begin to form simple sentences, sometimes using punctuation.

Talk About
Talk about typical scenes that we see at Harvest time. Discuss the equipment that the farmer uses to harvest the crops and talk about the activities and objects that we might see in the fields.

Further Ideas
● Encourage the children to join in singing an extended version of the rhyme 'It's Harvest time today!' on page 35, by increasing the number of bales in the first verse.
● Label a Harvest-themed collage showing drawings, photographs, magazine pictures and paintings of festival food and gifts.
● Take the children on a visit to a local 'Pick-your-own' farm, an allotment or garden vegetable patch.

Mathematical development

HARVEST TRAIL

Early Learning Goal
Say and use number names in order in familiar contexts.

Talk About
Talk with the children about the fruit and vegetables that we traditionally associate with Harvest time. Encourage them to name and identify the fruit and vegetables that you have cut in half for the activity.

What you need
A strip of card for each child, approximately 20cm by 50cm; shallow trays; poster paints; a selection of fruit and vegetables such as apples, pears, potatoes and carrots (an adult should cut these in half lengthways); sticky labels; small card discs; pens; dice.

What to do
● Provide each child with a long strip of card, paint in shallow trays and several half-sections of fruit and vegetables. Encourage the children to use the fruit and vegetable sections to create a colourful row of ten Harvest-themed prints. Put these aside to dry.
● Help the children to write the numbers 1 to 10 on to ten sticky labels and to position them, in numerical order, on to the ten prints that they have made to create a Harvest-themed gameboard.
● Give each child two small card discs and ask them to decorate them to make counters.
● Invite pairs of children to take turns to throw a dice and to move the counters along the gameboard. The first player to move their counter all the way to number 10 and then back again is the winner! Alternatively, just play for fun!

HARVEST BASKETS

Early Learning Goal
Find one more or one less than a number from one to 10.

Talk About
As you sing the song, pause between verses to talk about how many items are left in each basket and to establish how many items are left in total.

What you need
The 'Harvest baskets' rhyme on page 35; ten items of fruit and vegetables shared between three baskets.

What to do
● Position the baskets of fruit and vegetables in a row.
● Sing the rhyme 'Harvest baskets' with the children. As you sing, invite one child at a time to remove one piece of fruit or one vegetable from one of the baskets. If, say, a pear is removed, everyone should sing: 'But one basket wobbled and a pear fell out'.
● Continue the song until there is nothing left in the baskets! Repeat so that everyone has a chance to remove an item from one of the baskets.

Mathematical development

THE APPLE STORE

Early Learning Goal
Talk about, recognise and recreate simple patterns.

Talk About
Use the display to introduce patterns. Ask questions such as, 'Can you find two identical patterns?'; 'Which patterns use two colours?'; 'Is there a pattern that uses all three colours?'.

What you need
A copy of the 'Apple store' photocopiable sheet on page 42; red, green and yellow pencils; a display board and table; real or pretend apples in red, yellow and green (if necessary, cut apple shapes from card and paint them).

What to do
● Give each child a copy of the 'Apple store' photocopiable sheet. Help them to decorate each row of apples using a different repeated pattern, for example, red/yellow/green or red/red/green.
● Arrange the patterns on a display board and place a selection of real or pretend apples on the table.
● Encourage the children to use the interactive display by copying the patterns using the different-coloured apples.
● Order the apples into a simple pattern with the children watching. Ask the children to shut their eyes while you take an apple away from the display. Can the children tell you which apple is missing?

HARVEST MUNCH!

Early Learning Goal
In practical activities and discussion begin to use the vocabulary involved in adding and subtracting.

Talk About
Ask the children to imagine not having enough food to eat. Talk about sharing and giving to those who have less than us.

Further Ideas
● Adapt the 'Harvest trail' game on page 12 for older children by asking the children to add the score on two dice or spinners showing the numbers 0 to 3.
● Simplify the 'Harvest baskets' activity on page 12 for younger children by using five baskets with one item of fruit or vegetable in each. Begin the song, 'There were five fruit and veg…'.
● Extend the 'Harvest munch!' game on this page by using up to 20 items of food.
● Use 'The apple store' activity on this page with small groups of younger children. Make an A3 copy of the photocopiable sheet and use it as a shared resource.

What you need
Old clean gloves (or socks); circles of felt and PVA glue (or sticky labels); a tray; ten items of real or pretend food; two dice showing number 1 to 6.

What to do
● Encourage the children to stick two felt 'eyes' on to the knuckle section of an old glove to create a simple puppet.
● Place ten items of real or pretend food on a tray.
● Ask the first player to throw both dice, then help them to subtract one score away from the other. That player should use their puppet to 'eat up' the resulting number of food items. For example, if they throw a 6 and a 4, then they can 'eat' two items of food! (In reality, the player should hide each item of munched food on their lap.)
● If both dice show the same number, then they cannot 'eat' any items.
● Continue taking turns until all of the food is gone.
● The winner is the puppet that has 'eaten' the most. Alternatively, just play for fun.

Knowledge and understanding of the world

Early Learning Goal
Select the tools and techniques they need to shape, assemble and join materials they are using.

Talk About
Talk about animals that could cause damage to crops, such as birds, rabbits and slugs. Consider what else might cause a bad harvest, for example, floods, drought, poor soil and crop disease.

POOR HARVEST

What you need
Play dough or Plasticine; a copy of the 'Who's eating my cabbage?' photocopiable sheet on page 43; a tray; coloured pens and pencils; a cardboard disc with a picture of a caterpillar on one side.

What to do
● Invite the children to make a total of ten caterpillar shapes using play dough or Plasticine.
● Give each child a copy of the photocopiable sheet and encourage them to colour in the cabbage then cut around the shape where indicated.
● Ask three children to sit in a circle, each holding their cabbage pictures. Place the caterpillars on a tray in the middle of the circle.
● Let the players take turns to flip the disc. If it lands on the side showing the caterpillar, that player can take one caterpillar to place on their cabbage.
● If it lands on the side without the caterpillar, they should pass the disc to the next player. Continue until there are no caterpillars left on the tray.
● The winner is the player with the fewest caterpillars on their cabbage!

NICE RIPE APPLES!

Early Learning Goal
Build and construct with a wide range of objects, selecting appropriate resources, and adapting their work where necessary.

Talk About
Encourage the children to describe what happens if an apple is knocked off the tip of a branch. Will it land with a little bump, like the apples in the song?

What you need
The song 'Nice ripe apples' on page 36; apple-shaped template, approximately 10cm in diameter (see illustration); red and green card; scissors; brown thread; sticky tape; a large twig with plenty of branches; pot of soil, sand or plaster.

Preparation
Secure the large twig firmly in the pot of soil, sand or plaster.

What to do
● Sing the song 'Nice Ripe Apples' with the children.
● Invite the children to draw around the apple-shaped template on the red and green card to make several apple shapes. Help

them cut slits where indicated and to slot the shapes together to create several 3-D apple shapes.
● Help the children to tape a loop of brown thread on to the top of each apple to represent a stalk.
● Invite the children to hang their apples on the branches of the twig to create a 3-D display about the song.

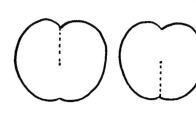

CROSS-CURRICULAR IDEAS

Knowledge and understanding of the world

HARVEST COLOURS

Early Learning Goal
Look closely at similarities, differences, patterns and change.

Talk About
Encourage the children to describe the change in appearance, texture, colour and smell of different types of fruit as they change. Use the display to help the children remember what happened.

What you need
A selection of very ripe fruit; plastic plate.

What to do
● Place a selection of very ripe fruit on a plastic plate.
● Over a period of time, encourage the children to observe the changes that happen to the fruit.
● Invite the children to make a series of close observational paintings or photographs as the food ripens, then ages.
● Display the pictures on the wall and help the children add simple labels describing the main changes, for example, 'The banana turned brown' or, 'The peach shrivelled up'.
● Tell the children that they can look at but not touch the fruit, and they must not under any circumstances eat any of it.

BEFORE HARVEST

Early Learning Goal
Find out about, and identify, some features of living things, objects and events they observe.

Talk About
Help the children gain an awareness of the work and effort that is needed before Harvest time by discussing what needs to be done in order to help plants to grow.

What you need
Young tomato plants; an area outside suitable for planting or patio pots; soil; fertiliser or plant food; children's gardening tools; paper; colouring materials; display area or blank Big Book (sheets of A3 paper stapled between a folded sheet of A2 card).

Preparation
Check for food allergies and dietary requirements.

What to do
● Set up a long-term activity by helping the children to plant some tomato plants in the ground or in patio pots outside. Encourage them to observe the plants regularly and to care for them by watering frequently and weeding if necessary.
● Talk with the children about the importance of sunshine and water in helping the plants to grow, and encourage them to notice changes in the size of the plant and colour of the fruit.
● When ripe, invite the children to pick and eat the tomatoes.
● Encourage the children to draw pictures showing how the tomatoes were grown from start to finish.
● Help the children to place the pictures in order along a display board or into a Big Book.

Further Ideas
● Find out about Harvest festivals in other parts of the world, such as 'Thanksgiving' in America and the Jewish festival of 'Sukkot'.
● Discuss how fridges, freezers and cans help us to keep food safe to eat for many months after Harvest.
● Find out about different fruits that grow on trees around the world, for example, apples, bananas, mangoes, pineapples, limes, coconuts, dates and guavas. If possible, buy samples from your local supermarket to observe, feel and smell.
● Find out about dried foods such as raisins, currants and sultanas, prunes, beans, peas, lentils and barley.
● Make a cake using dried fruit, or soup using dried beans, peas and lentils.

CROSS-CURRICULAR IDEAS

Physical development

THE CARROT COURSE

What you need
The rhyme 'Ten little carrots' on page 36; a safe, open area such as a hall; PE equipment including mats, tunnels and low benches; cardboard boxes; ten carrots (real or pretend).

What to do
● Encourage the children to join in as you say the rhyme 'Ten little carrots'.
● Set up a simple circular obstacle course in the hall to represent a vegetable patch.
● Place the ten carrots randomly around the course.
● Encourage the children to imagine they are the rabbits. Challenge them to find all of the carrots in the 'vegetable patch' by climbing up and over, round and through the obstacles.

> **Early Learning Goal**
> Travel around, under, over and through balancing and climbing equipment.

> **Talk About**
> Read and talk about some of the Beatrix Potter stories about rabbits who play around the vegetable patch in search of food.

APPLE JUMPING

What you need
A safe outdoor area; a cardboard box; pen; chalk.

What to do
● Invite the children to help you create an action-packed floor game. Using chalk, draw a row of ten large apple shapes on the ground outside. Make sure that each apple shape is one hop or jump away from the next.
● Encourage the children to make a giant dice by labelling a large cardboard box with the numbers 1, 2, 3, 1, 2, 3.
● Let the children take turns to roll the giant dice and to hop or jump along the same number of apple shapes. If a player lands on the same apple as someone else, both players must return to the beginning!
● The aim of the game is to be the first to reach the last apple. Alternatively, just play for fun!

> **Early Learning Goal**
> Show awareness of space, of themselves and of others.

> **Talk About**
> Use the 'Apple jumping' photocopiable sheet on page 44 to help the children create a simple board game based on the floor activity. Talk about rules and instructions for the board game.

ONE ONION, TWO TOMATOES!

Early Learning Goal
Use a range of small and large equipment.

Talk About
Encourage the children to consider how they could adapt the game for younger peers, for example, by carrying the items in a bag or basket.

What you need
For each team: a set of five pretend harvest items, for example, a play-food apple, loaf, egg, onion and tomato (ensure that each team has a similar set of items); a box; a safe area indoors or outside.

What to do
● This is a game for two or more teams of five players.
● Begin by placing five items of pretend Harvest produce in a box for each team. Place the box at one side of the space and ask the children to stand in their teams on the other side.
● On your signal, let the first team member run to their box, collect one item and carry it back to the second team member.
● The second team member must hold this item as they collect another and takes them both back to the third team member, and so on.
● If an item is dropped, that player must pick it up and carry on.
● The first team to collect all five items are the winners or, alternatively, just play for fun.

TRACTOR TRACKS

Early Learning Goal
Handle tools, objects, construction and malleable materials safely and with increasing control.

Talk About
Discuss how you could make the game more challenging by, for example, increasing the number of bales or racing against the clock.

Further Ideas
● Encourage the children to mime the actions of a tractor or combine harvester as it judders to a start, bumps over land, turns in the fields, tilts in gullies and stops with a shudder.
● Use the home corner for role-play scenarios about cooking a Harvest supper.
● Help the children to create model eggs using malleable materials such as clay or play dough. Place them in real egg boxes for 'sale' in a role-play farm shop.
● Invite the children to improvise an energetic scarecrow dance to instrumental music with fast and slow sections.

What you need
Large construction blocks; a safe area outdoors; sit-on wheeled toys.

Preparation
For each team, create a row of three large construction blocks in a safe area outdoors to represent bales of hay.

What to do
● Play this game in small teams of three or four children.
● Tell the children that the sit-on wheeled toys are farmyard vehicles and the construction blocks are hay bales.
● Give each team a wheeled toy and ask them to stand to one side of the 'farmyard'. Encourage the children in each team to take turns to manoeuvre their wheeled toy around all three 'bales' and back again.
● If any driver bumps into or knocks a 'bale' over, they must get off their vehicle and reposition the 'bale' before carrying on.
● The first complete team back to the farmyard are the winners or, alternatively, just play for fun.

Creative development

HAPPY HARVEST

What you need
Enlarged copies of the 'Happy Harvest' photocopiable sheet on page 46; tools and equipment for four different decorating techniques (for example, felt-tipped pens, coloured pencils, finger paints, fabric for collage, small squares of coloured paper for mosaic, pastels, glue and glitter); scissors.

Preparation
Make an enlarged copy of the 'Happy Harvest' sheet for each child.

What to do
● Give each child an enlarged copy of the 'Happy Harvest' photocopiable sheet.
● Encourage the children to cut out and decorate each picture using a different media to create a selection of colourful Harvest-themed gift tags.
● Help the children to write a 'Happy Harvest' message on the back of their tags, then invite them to attach their tags to the Harvest festival produce that is brought in for your Harvest festival service.

Early Learning Goal Explore colour, texture, shape, form and space in two or three dimensions.

Talk About Discuss the tradition of sharing Harvest produce with other people after a special Harvest festival service.

HARD-WORKING FARMERS

What you need
The song 'I saw three farmers working hard!' on page 37; percussion instruments.

What to do
● In one session, enjoy singing the song 'I saw three farmers working hard!' with the children. Sing it together several times, then invite the children to improvise music using simple percussion instruments.
● In a subsequent session, recap on the song, then encourage the children to consider the actions of a busy farmer in the past. Talk about swinging a scythe, bending for crops, tying up bales and cleaning tools.
● Invite two groups of children to take turns to mime the actions of a busy farmer, while the other children sing the song and play the instruments.

Early Learning Goal Recognise and explore how sounds can be changed, sing simple songs from memory, recognise repeated sounds and sound patterns and match movements to music.

Talk About Talk about the movements of a modern farmer, for example, climbing high into a combine harvester, driving a tractor and cleaning and mending large machinery.

Creative development

HARVEST TIME

What you need
Copies of, or books containing copies of, Harvest-themed paintings (for example, *Peasant woman cutting straw*; *The Thresher*; *The Sheaf-Binder* and *Harvest in Provence* by Van Gogh and *The Threshing Machine* and *The Gleaners* by C Pissarro); very thick paints; painting equipment; card or thick paper.

What to do
● Show the children copies of Harvest-themed paintings featuring traditional scenes from the past.
● Encourage the children to look at the scenes carefully and to describe what is happening.
● Challenge the children to make up short stories or scenarios about the people in the pictures, then invite them to recreate these scenes or stories in mime or role-play.
● In a subsequent session, encourage the children to paint a picture about the scenes or stories, using thick paints to recreate the textured style of Van Gogh.

HARVEST BOWL

What you need
Five newspapers; PVA glue; bucket; water; wooden spoon; plastic bowl (to be used as a mould); cling film; poster paints; paintbrushes.

What to do
● Invite the children to make some special bowls in which to display produce for your Harvest festival.
● Ask the children to tear the newspapers into narrow strips. Let the children place the strips in a bucket and cover with water. Then leave to soak overnight.
● The next day, squeeze out the excess water and add two cups of PVA glue. Mix together with a wooden spoon.
● Cover the upturned bowl with cling film. Encourage the children to firmly press small handfuls of the mixture all over the cling film, then leave to dry thoroughly. (This might take three or four days!)
● When dry, carefully remove the bowl from the mould and invite the children to cover the surface with white paint.
● After this has dried, let the children paint the bowl with abstract patterns using Harvest-themed colours.

● Help the children to create observational paintings of Harvest-themed produce. Mount and display the pictures with examples of the real items.
● Look at a selection of colourful stamps. Invite the children to design a Harvest-themed stamp. Display the designs in a role-play post office.
● Help the children to print or paint cross-sections of fruit on to white fabric. When dry, use the fabric to make aprons, cushions or simple curtains for the home corner.
● Help the children to create colour-wash Harvest scenes by using thick yellow wax crayon to draw streaks of corn blowing in a field. Brush a weak solution of blue paint over the wax to represent sky.

CRAFT AND GIFT IDEAS

Personal, social and emotional development

Early Learning Goal
Understand that people have different needs, views, cultures and beliefs, that need to be treated with respect.

Group Size
Small groups.

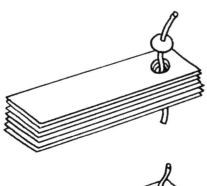

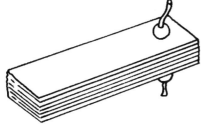

Support and Extension
Help younger children to punch the holes and tie the beads. Encourage older children to help cut out the nine strips of card.

Further Ideas
● Encourage the children to decorate the strips of card before they make the basket.
● If possible take the children to meet the recipients of their Harvest goods and gift baskets.
● Invite the children to make more baskets to take home as a gift for someone special, a sick friend or relative, or someone who needs cheering up.

GIFT BASKETS

What you need

For each child: nine strips of card (approximately 4cm by 26cm); two 10cm lengths of string or ribbon each with a bead tied to one end; two spare beads; a child-safe hole-punch; PVA glue; real fruit and vegetables.

What to do

● Using the 'Background information and planning' on pages 5 and 6, help the children find out about the Harvest tradition of sharing the good things that they have with those in need.
● Invite the children to make a gift to give away after a Harvest festival service.
● In turn, help the children to use the hole-punch to make a hole at either end of seven of their nine strips of card.
● Place the seven strips in a pile on top of each other, then poke the beaded length of string or ribbon through all seven holes at one end of the pile.
● Tie a second bead on to the loose end of string underneath the pile. Repeat this process at the other end.
● Encourage the children to fan out the seven strips of card to make a basket shape.
● Help the children to spread PVA glue on to the eighth strip of card. Stick it across the inside of the basket to keep the shape rigid.
● Finally, help the children to glue the ninth strip of card across the top of the basket to create a decorative handle. Note: the handle is for decoration – it will not hold the weight of the fruit.
● Invite the children to fill their basket with fruit or vegetables to create a Harvest gift.

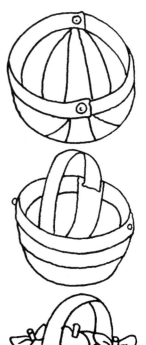

CRAFT AND GIFT IDEAS

Physical development

SHEAVES OF CORN

<table>
<tr><td>

Early Learning Goal

</td><td>

Move with control and coordination.

</td></tr>
</table>

Group Size

Pairs of children or small groups for the craft activity; small or large groups for the game.

What you need
The song 'In and out the sheaves of corn' on page 36. For the craft activity: samples of real corn (or colour pictures or photographs); thin yellow card (approximately A2 size); scissors; thick paint in shades of brown, white and yellow; thick paintbrushes; funnel; plastic bottles with screw lid; dry sand; string or yellow raffia. For the game: a large room or safe area outside.

Preparation
● Begin by singing 'In and out the sheaves of corn' together. Explain that the children are going to help make the components for a 'Follow-my-leader' style game, based on the words in the song.

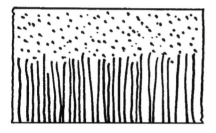

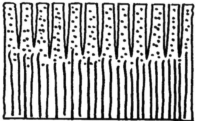

What to do
● Give small groups or pairs of children a large sheet of yellow card.
● Help them to mix a little brown paint with some yellow and white paint to make a colour that is similar to real corn.
● Encourage the children to use thick brush strokes to create repeated and overlapping streaks of paint across the whole sheet of card.
● Decorate the top half of the painting by repeatedly dabbing thick spots of paint randomly over the streaks, to represent a field of corn blowing in the breeze.
● When it is completely dry, help the children to cut several slits in the painting
● Trim the tip of each strip of card to create rounded ends – this does not need to look perfect, rough cutting if fine!
● Encourage the children to use a funnel to fill a plastic bottle with sand, then screw the lid on firmly.
● Help the children to wrap the painting around the bottle. Tie it firmly around the middle with string or yellow raffia to create a 3-D, freestanding model of a sheaf of corn.
● Stand several 'sheaves of corn' models around a room or safe area outside to represent a harvested field.
● Invite the children to sing the song 'In and out the sheaves of corn', as they take turns to be the leader weaving in and out of the structures pretending to be butterflies or other flying creatures.
● If any of the 'sheaves' are knocked over, the children should stop and reposition them.

Support and Extension

Help younger children with the cutting and tying stages. Encourage older children to decorate both sides of the card to create a more realistic effect.

Further Ideas

● Invite the children to reposition the sheaves of corn to create different routes for the game, for example, a row, a circle, a wavy line or random positions.
● Encourage the children to use actions such as hopping, jumping and skipping as they play the game.

Personal, social and emotional development

HARVEST LOAF

What you need

Ingredients: 575g wholemeal flour; one tsp salt; one tsp caster sugar; 12g butter; 25g fresh yeast; 300ml lukewarm water; 150ml lukewarm milk; salted water.

Equipment: oven (adult use); large plastic bowl; small plastic bowl; wooden board; baking tray; wire rack.

Preparation

Check for food allergies and dietary requirements. Wash hands and put on aprons. Make sure surfaces are clean.

What to do

● Invite the children to work together to make a special Harvest loaf.

● Begin by sifting the flour into a large bowl. Add the salt and sugar and rub in the butter.

● In a separate bowl, mix the yeast with a little warm water until it is creamy.

● Mix the dry ingredients with the creamy yeast, milk and enough water to create a firm dough.

● Place on a floured board and knead for about ten minutes.

● Cover and leave for 30 to 40 minutes or until it has doubled in size.

● Knead well then divide the dough into six pieces, leaving a little spare for decoration. Roll each piece into a long, narrow sausage shape.

● Help the children to place five lengths of dough close together side by side, to represent a bundle of corn. Wrap the sixth length around the middle.

● Fan out the five lengths. Make tiny balls from the spare dough and press these across the top of the sausage lengths (see illustration).

● Place on a large buttered baking tray and gently press the shapes together. Brush with salted water.

● Cover and leave to rise for about 30 to 40 minutes.

● Bake at 230°C, 450°F or gas mark 8 for 40 to 45 minutes. Leave to cool on a wire rack

● Display the bread at your Harvest festival service or invite the children to use the bread to make sandwiches for a party or picnic to celebrate 'Harvest-home' or 'Thanksgiving' (see 'Hold your own celebration' on pages 28 and 29).

Early Learning Goal

Work as part of a group or class, taking turns and sharing fairly, understanding that there needs to be agreed values and codes of behaviour for groups of people, including adults and children, to work together harmoniously.

Group Size

Small groups.

Support and Extension

Help younger children on a one-to-one basis. Encourage older children to use their observations of real traditional Harvest loaves to help them add extra details such as snips, twists and plaits.

Further Ideas

● Encourage the children to model a tiny dough mouse to add to their loaf prior to baking.

● Find out why a mouse shape was often used to decorate Harvest loaves (see 'Background information and planning' on pages 5 and 6).

COOKERY IDEAS

SEASONAL SOUP

Early Learning Goal Interact with others, negotiating plans and activities and taking turns in conversation.

Group Size Small groups.

What you need

Ingredients: one carrot; one parsnip; half a turnip; one onion; two celery stalks; one leek; 25g butter; 800ml water; one tbsp well-washed barley; one tsp salt.
Equipment: cooker (adult use); saucepan; spatula; jug; two large plastic bowls; sharp knife (adult use); serving bowl; ladle; small plastic soup bowls; spoons.

Preparation

Check for food allergies and dietary requirements. Wash hands and put on clean aprons.

What to do

● Invite the children to work together to make a tasty seasonal soup.

● Encourage them to help wash the vegetables, inviting discussion about why they need to be washed before being used.
● Ask the children to be in charge of the vegetables, holding them in a large plastic bowl and handing you one vegetable at a time for you to prepare. Challenge them to name each vegetable as they hand it to you.
● Explain that the carrot, parsnip and turnip need to be diced, the onion and celery need to be chopped and the leek needs to be shredded. Can anyone suggest why the vegetables need to be cut up?
● After you have prepared each vegetable, invite the children to tip the pieces into a large plastic bowl.
● With the children at a safe distance from the heat source, melt the butter in a saucepan and add the prepared vegetables. Cover the pan.
● Fry the vegetables gently, without browning, for about seven minutes.
● Encourage the children to watch as you pour in the water and add the barley and salt.
● Bring the soup to the boil. Lower the heat, cover the pan and simmer gently for about one and a half hours, or until the barley is soft.
● Talk about the different stages of the recipe up to this point. While your soup is cooking, invite the children to draw and write about the ingredients and recipe.
● When the soup is ready, remove the saucepan from the heat and pour the soup into a large serving bowl to cool.
● Ladle into small bowls for the children to enjoy.

Support and Extension Help younger children to name the vegetables. Encourage older children to help weigh and measure the butter, water, barley and salt.

Further Ideas
● Use the children's pictures to create a recipe booklet.
● Place a selection of raw vegetables in a covered box. Play a game by asking the children to take turns to describe one of the vegetables for their peers to name and identify.

Mathematical development

MICHAELMAS DAISY NUMBER LINE

What you need

A long display board at the children's own height; blue, green and yellow paints; paintbrushes; ten sheets of paper (A4 or A3 size); glue; examples or pictures of a Michaelmas daisy if possible.

Preparation

Help the children to label ten sheets of paper with bold numerals from 1 to 10.

What to do

● Talk to the children about 'Michaelmas' (see 'Background information and planning' on pages 5 and 6). Explain that a pretty flower called the Michaelmas daisy usually bloomed at the same time as the Michaelmas celebrations.

● If possible, look at examples or pictures of a Michaelmas daisy with the children. Alternatively, explain that the flower resembles a blue daisy with a yellow centre and small green leaves.

● Provide the children with the ten sheets of numbered paper and paints in blue, yellow and green. Invite them to paint one simple flower on the first sheet to represent one Michaelmas daisy, two flowers on the second sheet and so on up to ten flowers on the last sheet.

● Mount the pictures in the correct order to create a giant floral number line.

● Encourage the children to use the number line as a visual resource for counting 'one more' by singing the following rhyme, to the tune of 'Five Currant Buns' (Traditional):

One little daisy sitting in a line
Blue and yellow at Harvest time
Up popped another with the sun and rain
That made one more, let us count again!

● Start the second verse with the words 'Two little daisies', and so on, continuing up to ten.

● When the children are comfortable with this, use the number line as a visual resource for counting 'one less' by singing:

Ten little daisies sitting in a line
Blue and yellow at Harvest time
One was picked by the children in the lane
That made one less, let us count again!

● Start the second verse with 'Nine little daisies' and so on, counting down again.

Communication, language and literacy

HARVEST OFFERINGS

What you need

Plain white card cut into the shape of a traditional church window, approximately 100cm by 50cm, cut into equal pieces, one per child; thick soft felt-tipped pens; thick black permanent marker; the story 'Loaves and fishes' on page 32; pictures or photographs of stained glass windows.

Preparation

If possible, take the children to a local church to observe the stained glass windows.

Group Size Small or large groups.

What to do

● Explain to the children that, in the past, people offered whatever they could for the Harvest festival church service as a way of saying 'thank you' to God for the produce obtained from the land. For example, in mining towns, some of the miners would offer coal.

● In some coastal towns and villages, fishermen would offer a selection of the fish that they caught to their local seaside church as a way of saying 'thank you' to God for the harvest of the sea.

● Read the story often told at Harvest time about how Jesus fed five thousand people with just five loaves and fishes.

● Provide each child with a piece of shaped card. Invite the children to use a permanent marker to decorate the card with thick black lines, to resemble leading on a stained glass window.

Support and Extension Help younger children by drawing the fish shapes on to the card for them to fill in with colourful patterns such as stripes, dots, circles and crosses. Encourage older children to decorate the fish with more intricate patterns.

● Encourage the children to use the thick felt-tipped pens to draw shoals of colourful fish in between the black lines. Help them to fill small gaps with blue wavy lines to represent the sea water.

● Position the card scenes high up on a wall to create a beautiful 'Harvest offerings' display in the style of a large stained glass window.

Further Ideas
● Use thin fabric and fabric paints instead of card and felt-tipped pens. Display the finished designs against a window so that the light shines through them.
● Use the 'Loaves and fishes' photocopiable sheet on page 46 to play 'Snap' or 'Pairs'.
● Help the children to cut out and decorate card fish shapes. Attach thread to the shapes and suspend them in groups to resemble shoals of fish.

ROLE-PLAY IDEAS

Knowledge and understanding of the world

PEARLY KINGS AND QUEENS

Early Learning Goal

Investigate objects and materials by using all of their senses as appropriate.

Group Size

Small or large groups.

What you need

Card shapes, such as ovals, hearts, diamonds and squares (approximately 10cm wide or long); child-safe hole-punch; lengths of wool measuring 5cm to 15cm); pearl buttons (white buttons, white beads or fake pearls with large holes); sticky-backed Velcro; masking tape; dressing-up clothes such as hats, dresses, skirts, trousers, waistcoats and jackets; home corner or role-play area; full-length mirror.

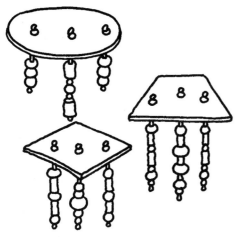
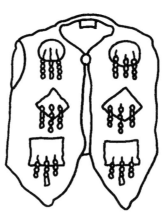

What to do

● Using the 'Background information and planning' on pages 5 and 6, remind the children about the links between Pearly kings and queens and Harvest time.

● Invite the children to turn old clothes into pearly outfits for some dressing-up fun.

● Encourage the children to select card shapes and then to punch three to five holes in each shape. The position of the holes is unimportant.

● Next, help them to thread a selection of pearl buttons, white beads or fake pearls on to pre-cut lengths of wool.

● Help the children to thread the strings of pearls through the holes in the card, so that they dangle freely. Secure the wool at the back using masking tape.

Support and Extension

Help younger children with the fiddly stages such as threading and knotting. Encourage older children to cut out a selection of different card shapes.

● Invite the children to use Velcro to attach their pearly decorations to dressing-up clothes.

● Place a full-length mirror and the decorated outfits in the home corner. Encourage the children to dress up as Pearly kings, queens and princesses for spontaneous role-play.

Further Ideas

● Encourage the children to join in short and simple role-play scenarios based on getting ready for the Harvest festival.

● Help the children to make a bouquet or basket of real or pretend vegetables using decorative wrapping such as tissue paper, ribbons and bows.

Mathematical development

Use developing mathematical ideas and methods to solve practical problems.

Group Size
Small groups.

SEASONAL SALES

What you need
Low-level tables; green fabric or paper; real or pretend fruit and vegetables; shallow open-topped boxes or wicker baskets; real or pretend money; price labels made from small pieces of folded card; thick pens; toy till or small box; paper bags.

What to do
● Explain to the children that many farmers sell their produce at special markets during Harvest time.

Support and Extension
Help younger children to identify the different coins and work out the change that they will need. Encourage older children to write more complex labels such as, 'Half price', 'Two for the price of one' and, 'Buy one get one free'.

Further Ideas
● Provide dressing-up clothes for the role-play area so that the children feel in character.
● Encourage the children to draw colourful posters to advertise the produce and prices at the farmers' market. Use the posters to decorate the role-play area.
● Talk about healthy foods and the importance of a balanced diet.
● Use information books to find out about Harvest produce grown in other countries.

● Invite the children to help set up pretend fruit and vegetable stalls in the role-play area to create a farmers' market.
● Cover low-level tables with green fabric or paper and invite the children to display real or pretend produce in rows of open-topped boxes or baskets.
● Help the children to write a selection of price labels on small pieces of folded card to stand by the boxes, for example, '5p each', 'Two for 10p', '15p for 3' and so on.
● Place some paper bags and a money box or toy till containing real or pretend coins on each stall.
● Invite small groups of children to use the farmers' market for role-play situations, taking turns to 'buy' and 'sell' the produce. Help them solve practical problems. For example, 'How many apples can you afford with the coins that you have?'; 'Which coins should you use?'; 'How much change will you need?'.

Creative development

HARVEST ASSEMBLY

Early Learning Goal
Explore colour, texture, shape, form and space in two or three dimensions.

Group Size
Small or large groups.

What you need
A traditional or digital camera that the children can use; A5 card or paper in autumnal colours such as orange, brown, beige, yellow and red; child-safe hole-punch; wide silky ribbon; glue or double-sided sticky tape.

Preparation
Ask parents and carers if their children could bring in a photograph album showing pictures of a special event or celebration that they have attended, such as a birthday party, a wedding or a festival. Seek parental permission to take photographs of the children.

What to do
● Explain to the children that people often take photographs to help record special events and celebrations.
● Encourage the children to show their peers the photograph albums that they have brought from home, and to talk about the special events that they show.
● Tell the children that they are going to use the traditional or digital camera to record the events before, during and after your Harvest festival.
● Prior to your festival, let the children take turns to use the camera to take photographs of their peers bringing Harvest baskets into the venue or helpers setting up the Harvest display.

> Preparing for our Harvest festival

● Help them to take photographs during the celebration to show people singing or listening attentively to a speaker.
● After the festival, let them take turns to photograph helpers dismantling the Harvest display or their peers donating the produce to local worthy causes.
● When the photographs are processed or retrieved from the printer, invite the children to sort them into three groups that show events before, during and after the Harvest celebrations.

Support and Extension
Help younger children on a one-to-one basis as they take the photographs. Encourage older children to experiment by taking photographs at unusual angles or different distances.

● Help the children to use card or paper in autumnal colours and a hole-punch and ribbon to create three simple photograph albums.
● Encourage them to display the photographs and to decorate the front cover of each album as a record of their festival.
● Let the children refer back to the completed albums over time to remind themselves of Harvest.

Further Ideas
● Invite the children to draw or paint three Harvest-themed pictures or mini-collages to decorate the front cover of each photograph album.
● Encourage the children to write simple captions describing the scene or naming the people in each photograph.
● Let the children use colourful felt-tipped pens or pencils to create a decorative border around the photographs in each album.
● Make a selection of photograph albums recording other special festivals and celebrations in your setting during the year.

HOLD YOUR OWN CELEBRATION

Knowledge and understanding of the world

Early Learning Goal
Begin to know about their own cultures and beliefs and those of other people.

Group Size
Small or large groups.

THANKSGIVING

What you need
Bread (for example, the Harvest loaf that you made in the Cookery activity on page 22); butter; blunt knife; plastic plates; sliced turkey; cranberry sauce; clean tablecloths; fresh flowers; shatter-proof vases; pretty napkins; American flag; triangles of paper; red and blue pens; string; sticky tape; party clothes.

Preparation
Check for food allergies and dietary requirements. Ask parents and carers if they can help by donating or preparing party food.

What to do
● Using the 'Background information and planning' on pages 5 and 6 for reference, discuss the American celebration of Thanksgiving with the children.
● Explain that American families celebrate Thanksgiving with a special meal – usually turkey with cranberry sauce and vegetables – followed by pumpkin pie for pudding.
● Invite the children to help make turkey and cranberry sauce sandwiches for a party in honour of Thanksgiving, using the special Harvest loaf that you baked together if possible. Include other party foods donated by parents and carers.
● Encourage the children to hang up an American flag for the celebration and to help prepare tables for the party food using clean tablecloths, fresh flowers and pretty napkins.
● Help the children to decorate paper triangles with stars and stripes, then tape these on to lengths of string to create party banners.
● Suggest that the children wear party clothes and invite parents and carers to join in with your celebration.

Support and Extension
Provide younger children with one-to-one support as they make the sandwiches. Help older children to look in cookery books to find a recipe for pumpkin pie.

Further Ideas
● Make a pumpkin pie for the children to taste.
● Find out about other Harvest-themed festivals and celebrations from around the world, such as Shavuot, a Jewish festival that used to be called the 'Feast of the Harvest'; Pongal, a Hindu festival that celebrates the sugar-cane harvest or the Japanese Lantern Festival, which celebrates the rice harvest.

Physical development

<table>
<tr><td>Early Learning Goal</td><td>Move with confidence, imagination and in safety.</td></tr>
<tr><td>Group Size</td><td>Small or large groups.</td></tr>
</table>

SCARECROW DANCE

What you need

The song 'Head, shoulders, knees and toes – I am free!' on page 37; a safe, open area; pictures of scarecrows.

What to do

● Show the children the pictures of scarecrows. Explain that farmers used to put scarecrows in their fields to scare birds away from their crops.

● Ask, 'Have you ever seen a scarecrow in a field or allotment?'; 'Why would a bird be afraid of a scarecrow?'; 'How is a scarecrow made?'.

● Invite the children to join in as you sing the song, 'Head, shoulders, knees and toes – I am free!'. Explain that the song is about an imaginary scarecrow, who is set free from his pole!

● Encourage the children to think about how the scarecrow would move with limp and loose limbs.

● Discuss the movements using descriptive words such as 'flopping', 'flapping', 'dangling', 'stumbling', 'tripping', 'spinning', 'twirling', 'turning', 'bending' and 'twisting'.

● Encourage the children to mime the movements, imagining that they are scarecrows who have been set free from their poles.

● Invite the children to focus on three favourite movements, for example, stumbling, twirling and twisting or flopping, tripping and spinning.

Support and Extension

Help younger children by prompting descriptive words to describe the movements of the scarecrow. Encourage older children to perform their sequence of movements in front of an audience such as peers and staff or parents and carers.

Further Ideas

● Play some instrumental music with fast and slow sections for the children to dance to.

● Invite the children to work in pairs or small groups to create 'Follow-my-leader' style dances.

● Encourage the children to paint a picture showing a scarecrow dancing in a field.

● Work together to create a life-sized scarecrow using old clothes stuffed with newspaper or straw.

● Encourage them to put these three movements together to create a short dance sequence. Choose individuals to perform their routines in front of the others.

● Invite the children to sing the song aloud as they perform their dance sequences. Emphasise the importance of moving around the room safely, looking out for other dancers and avoiding collisions.

Creative development

Use their imagination in art and design, music, dance, imaginative role-play and stories.

Small or large groups.

HARVEST MICE

What you need
A safe, open space; the 'Harvest mouse' photocopiable sheet on page 47; coloured pens and pencils; paint and paintbrushes; collage materials; scissors; wool or ribbon; instrumental music; music-playing facilities; information books containing pictures of harvest mice.

What to do
● Share the pictures of harvest mice with the children. Use the information books to find out about the mice. For example: how big are they? What colour are they? Where do they live? What do they eat? Why are they called 'Harvest mice'?
● Give each child a copy of the 'Harvest mouse' photocopiable sheet.
● Help the children to cut around the dotted lines and to cut out the eyeholes.
● Encourage a high degree of independence as the children decorate the mask using collage materials, paints, pens or pencils.
● Help the children to add wool or ribbon ties.
● Encourage the children to think of words to describe the movements of a mouse, for example, 'scurry', 'skip', 'scamper', 'run', 'climb', 'jump', 'twitch', 'dart', 'twist', 'turn', 'scratch' and 'roll'.
● Invite the children to wear their mouse masks as they mime the movements of the animal in a safe, open space.
● Play some instrumental music for the children to move to. Include music that has fast and slow sections to inspire the children to use a varied range of actions.

Help younger children by prompting words to describe the movements of a mouse and make sure that they understand what the words mean. Encourage pairs or small groups of older children to take turns to perform a short sequence of movements for their peers to watch.

● Encourage pairs or small groups of children to make up a short sequence of movements to perform to music.
● Invite the children to write or tell short stories about imaginary harvest mice. Suggest simple titles as starting points, for example, 'The lost mouse', 'The runaway mouse' or 'Dancing mice'. Encourage them to act out their short stories or scenarios in the role-play area.
● Challenge the children to use malleable materials to create 3-D models of Harvest mice or imaginary creatures that live in fields of corn.

LOAVES AND FISHES

Jesus was with his disciples on a hill above Lake Galilee. A large crowd of people were making their way towards him. Jesus understood how weary and hungry everybody would be after travelling a long way to see him.

Jesus asked Philip, one of the disciples, 'Where can we buy enough food to feed all these people?'

Philip thought carefully then replied, 'To buy only a little bread for each person here would cost more than two hundred silver coins!'

A farm worker would only earn one of these coins for a hard day's labour, so two hundred coins was an enormous amount of money.

Another disciple stepped towards Jesus and said, 'There is a boy carrying five loaves of barley bread and two fish, but that wouldn't be enough to feed every person here!'

Jesus knew differently. He held the loaves and fish and thanked God for them. Jesus then began to share out the food. Amazingly, there was more than enough to feed everyone!

Jesus waited until everybody had finished eating. He then asked the twelve disciples to collect any leftover bread. Miraculously, there was enough bread left to fill 12 baskets!

There is a strong message in this story. We should all be willing to share what we have, even if we only have very little ourselves. The boy in this story is a good example of this. He only had five loaves of bread and two fishes, but he was still willing to share it out with everybody around him. Perhaps other people in the crowd had a little food. Seeing the boy's generosity might have encouraged them to share what they had. The disciples were even able to gather leftover food when everyone had finished eating. This helps to remind us how precious food is, and how wasteful it is to throw good food away.

JOSEPH AND HIS BROTHERS

There are strong messages in this Bible story.

Through careful planning, Joseph was able to save food when the harvests were good. This meant that, when the harvests were poor, there was still enough to feed everyone. Are there people we can share our food with today?

Joseph forgave his brothers even though they had treated him badly in the past. Joseph offered to share his food with them. This reminds us of the importance of forgiveness. What should we say if we have done something wrong?

There was once a boy called Joseph who had eleven brothers. Joseph's father gave him a very special coat for his birthday. It was a wonderful coat of many colours and it made Joseph feel important. But Joseph's older brothers were very jealous.

One day Joseph told his brothers that he dreamed they were tying up sheaves of corn at Harvest time when, suddenly, the brothers' bundles of corn all flopped over and bowed to Joseph's bundle of corn! The brothers listened to Joseph's dream but were very cross, and said that they would never bow down to Joseph as if he were more important than them.

One day, the brothers were very cruel and unkind. They tore Joseph's coat off his back and pushed Joseph into an empty well. Then they sent Joseph away to work for some strangers. The brothers went home with the torn coat and told their father that Joseph was dead. Joseph's father, Jacob, was heartbroken.

As time went by, things got even worse for Joseph. He was put in prison for something he had not done. While he was in prison, Joseph spent his time telling people what their dreams meant.

One night, Joseph was taken to the King and asked to listen to his strange

dreams. One of the dreams was about seven thin grains of corn that swallowed up seven fat grains of corn. But the thin corn did not get any bigger! Joseph explained that the dream meant there

JOSEPH AND HIS BROTHERS

was going to be seven years of good harvest followed by seven years of bad harvest, when the people would go hungry.

The King thought that Joseph was very clever to understand his dreams. Joseph was let out of prison and was asked to prepare for the bad harvest. He worked hard storing food during the good harvest and saved enough food to keep everyone alive during the bad harvest.

Many miles away, Joseph's brothers and father were starving because of the poor harvest. The brothers went to look for food and arrived at the place were Joseph lived. They did not recognise Joseph. They all bowed down to Joseph and asked if they could buy some food. Joseph recognised his brothers and realised his 'bowing' dream had come true. Joseph discovered that the brothers were very sorry for how they treated him all those

years ago and found out that they were no longer cruel and unkind. Joseph forgave his brothers and asked them to go and tell their father that he was still alive! Joseph invited the whole family to stay with him and to share the food that he had stored so that they would not go hungry during the years of bad harvest.

Round and round the hay barn

(Sung to the tune of 'Round and Round the Garden')

Round and round the hay barn
Looking everywhere;
One stack, two stacks,
Hay stacks everywhere!

It's Harvest time today!

(Sung to the tune of 'Sing a Song of Sixpence')

Sing a song of autumn,
It's Harvest time today;
Lots and lots of growing corn
And five big bales of hay.
When a bale was opened,
The hay flew everywhere;
Now look at all that scattered hay
It's floating in the air!

(Repeat, counting down to 'four big bales of hay', then 'three big bales of hay' and so on.)

Harvest baskets

(Sung to the tune of 'There Were Ten in a Bed')

There were ten fruit and veg,
In baskets on the ledge;
At Harvest, at Harvest!
But one basket wobbled and a *(name of fruit or vegetable)* fell out.

There were nine fruit and veg...

Ten little carrots

Ten little carrots, hiding here and there,
Rabbits in the veggie patch, please take care!
Climbing up and over
Round and through,
Nine little carrots are left for you!

Nine little carrots, hiding here and there...

Nice ripe apples

(Sung to the tune of 'Here We Go Round the Mulberry Bush')

Nice ripe apples falling down, falling down, falling down;
Nice ripe apples falling down; landing bump-bump on the ground.

Green and red with stalks of brown, stalks of brown, stalks of brown;
Green and red with stalks of brown; landing bump-bump on the ground.

In and out the sheaves of corn

(Sung to the tune of 'In and Out the Dusty Bluebells')

In and out the sheaves of corn,
In and out the sheaves of corn,
In and out the sheaves of corn,
Let's all dance together.

Flitter flutter; Flitter flutter; through the fields,
Flitter flutter; Flitter flutter; through the fields,
Flitter flutter; Flitter flutter; through the fields,
Let's all dance together.

HARVEST
RHYMES

I saw three farmers working hard!

(Sung to the tune of 'I Saw Three Ships Come Sailing By')

I saw three farmers working hard,
Working hard, working hard.
I saw three farmers working hard,
At Harvest time in the autumn.

And what do you think they were doing then,
Doing then, doing then?
And what do you think they were doing then,
At Harvest time in the autumn?

They were gathering crops and corn,
Crops and corn, crops and corn,
They were gathering crops and corn,
At Harvest time in the autumn.

Head, shoulders, knees and toes – I am free!

(Sung to the tune of 'Head, Shoulders, Knees and Toes')

Head, shoulders, knees and toes – I am free!
Head, shoulders, knees and toes – I am free!
Arms and legs and hands and nose,
Head, shoulders, knees and toes – I am free!

THE FRIENDLY SCARECROW

● Cut out the six pictures and stick them in the correct order.

MR SCARECROW

- Label a wooden brick with the letters 'y', 'b', 'r', 'o', 'p' and 'g'.

- Take turns to throw the dice and colour in one section with any colour that begins with that letter. For example, 'b' could be blue, black, brown or beige.

HARVEST POEM

Thank you

for the sun and rain.

Thank you

for the corn and grain.

Thank you

for the gathered wheat.

Thank you

for the food we eat.

HARVEST RECIPE

- Write about the ingredients or recipe.

_____

_____

_____

_____

_____

_____

_____

HARVEST
APPLE STORE

● Use two or three colours to create repeated patterns.

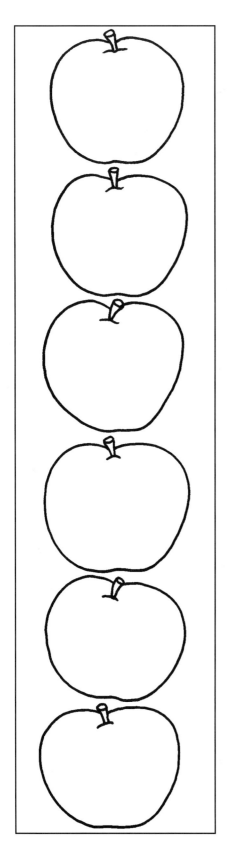
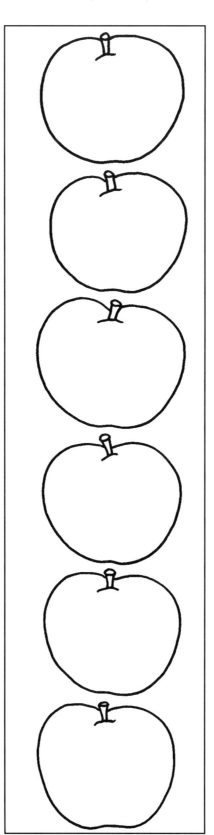
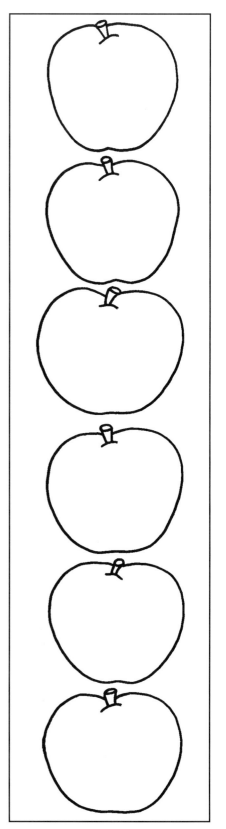

WHO'S EATING MY CABBAGE?

● Colour in and cut out the cabbage.

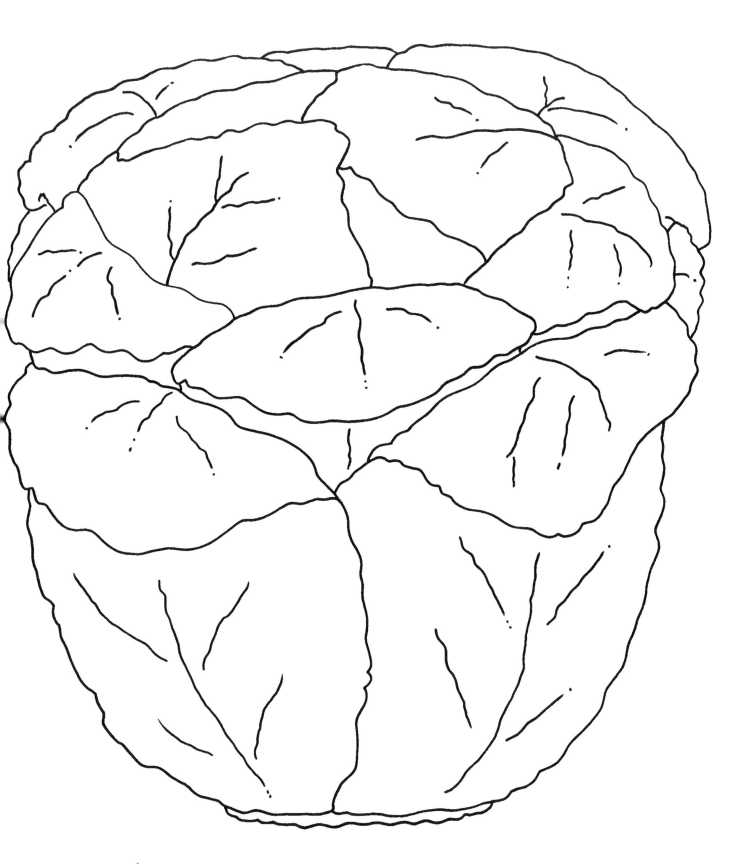

HARVEST
APPLE JUMPING

- Colour the Harvest items.

- Throw a dice and move your counter by following the arrows. If you land on an apple, jump forward one space. The winner is the first to reach the 'finish'.

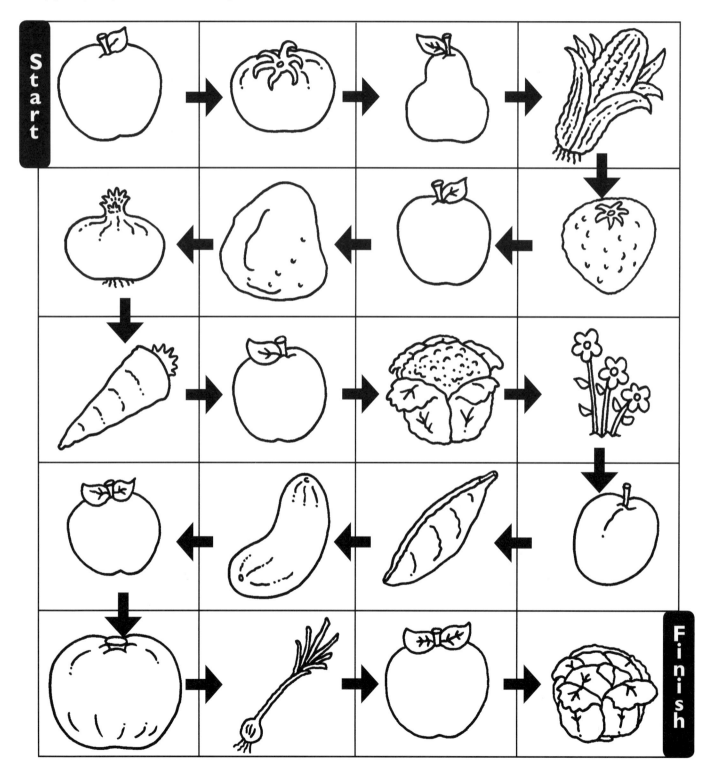

● Colour in and cut out the gift tags.

HARVEST
LOAVES AND FISHES

● Make several copies. Cut out the pictures.

● Use to play 'Snap', 'Pairs' or to make up your own matching game.

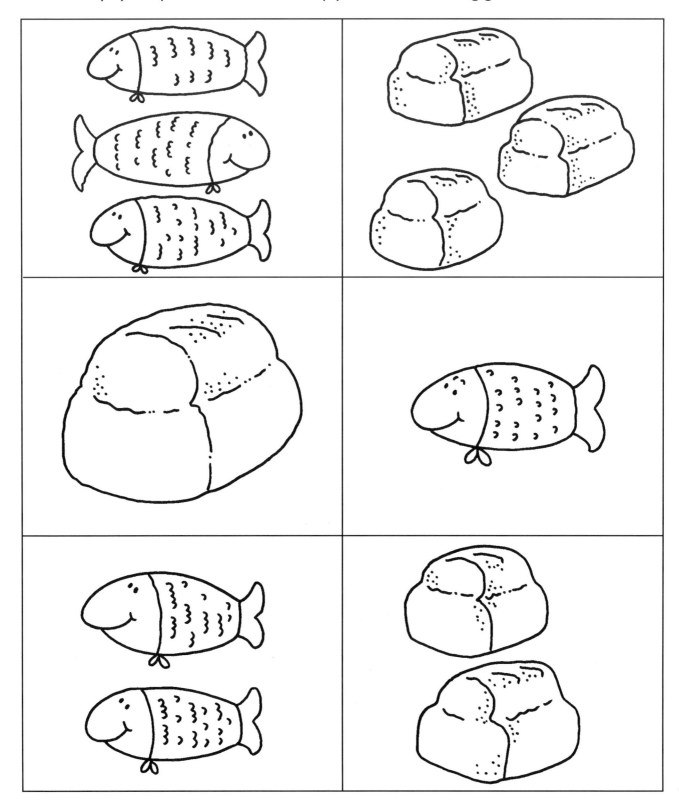

- Colour in and cut out the mask.

- Tape on ribbon ties and string whiskers.

RESOURCES

Story and picture books

The Enormous Turnip retold by Nicola Baxter (*Favourite Tales* series Ladybird)
Oliver's Vegetables by Vivian French (Hodder Children's Books)
Rosie Plants a Radish by Kate Petty (Macmillan Children's Books)
I Eat Vegetables! by Hannah Tofts (Zero to Ten)
Edward Plants a Garden by Dale Gottlieb (Tango Books)

Bible stories

First Bible Stories retold by Margaret Mayo (Orchard Books)
Joseph and His Brothers retold by Mary Auld (Franklin Watts)
Bible Stories for the Very Young by Sally Grindley (Bloomsbury Children's Books)

Information and activity books

Hunting, Harvesting and Home by Jacqueline Dineen (Belitha Press)
Festivals of the Christian Year by Lois Rock (Lion Publishing)
High Days and Holidays by David Self (Lion Publishing)

Song books

Harlequin: 44 Songs Around the Year by David Gadsby and Beatrice Harrap (A&C Black)

Equipment, games and role-play

Root Vue Farm contains a transparent grow tank, growing soil, vegetable seeds, plant labels, poster, instructions and a growing chart. Available from Insect Lore (PO Box 1420, Kiln Farm, Milton Keynes MK19 6ZH, tel: 01908 563338)
The Magnetic Healthy Food Fun Game has more than 30 magnetic pictures of healthy foods, other relevant materials and an information booklet. Available from NES Arnold (Novara House, Excelsior Road, Ashby de la Zouch, Leicestershire LE65 1NG, tel: 0845 1204525)
Mini Fruit Set and *Mini Vegetables Set* available from NES Arnold (Novara House, Excelsior Road, Ashby de la Zouch, Leicestershire LE65 1NG)
The Apple Number Line available from Hands On, Unit 11, Tannery Road, Tonbridge, Kent TN9 1RF, tel: 01732 225800

Poster sets

Christian Festivals available from Pictorial Charts Educational Trust (27 Kirchen Road, London W13 0UD, tel: 0208 5679206)
Fruit and Vegetable Poster Pack available from Hands On, Unit 11, Tannery Road, Tonbridge, Kent TN9 1RF, tel: 01732 225800

Websites

www.bbc.co.uk/religion
www.standards.dfes.gov.uk/schemes2/religion
www.request.org.uk
www.assemblies.org.uk
www.biblepicturegallery.com